VOID

Writers of Wales

EDITORS

MEIC STEPHENS   R. BRINLEY JONES

Some of the 'Cilie' poets and friends

From left to right:
Gerallt Jones, Dic Jones, David Jones (Isfoel),
Alun Jones, Simon B. Jones, T. Llew Jones, Tydfor Jones.

By kind permission of Mrs Ithel Davies, Penarth.

W. Rhys Nicholas

THE

FOLK POETS

University of Wales Press
on behalf of the Welsh Arts Council

1978

I

The literal translation of the Welsh term *bardd gwlad* is 'country poet', but such a term hardly serves to convey the wide connotation of the original. It may be true to say that no other term has evoked a more varied interpretation amongst literary critics in Wales during the last fifty years. As a result, its exact definition has become increasingly difficult. On the one hand, there are those who believe that the *bardd gwlad* has recently come to his own and that by now he is exerting a considerable influence on the Welsh poetic scene. There are others who maintain that there is no longer any justification for holding on to the concept of 'country poet', since there are very few today who aptly fit into the category it once represented. It seems, therefore, that for the purpose of this essay some attempt at definition is necessary, for this will evidently determine the scope of the discussion.

One literary critic who has attempted to give a comprehensive definition is Mr. Saunders Lewis. In 1939, in BANER AC AMSERAU CYMRU (March 22), he wrote a review on BEIRDD Y BABELL, an anthology of poems which had appeared in a popular 'poets' column', edited by Dewi Emrys in Y CYMRO. The date of that review is important for the reviewer draws attention to a significant change he had discerned in the contents of poems reputedly written by the *beirdd gwlad* of those days. In describing this change he delineates what gave to folk poetry its unique character:

The poets' column of yesteryear was, in its atmosphere and subjects, nearer to the news columns than it is at present. A poem to greet two on their wedding day, a memorial poem to another, verses to greet the first grand-daughter of an elderly grandmother, verses to welcome home a minister or church elder from hospital—those were the subjects that were common at one time, I believe, in the poetry columns of our local newspapers; they were read with the same interest as the prose news items from the same neighbourhoods. They were part of the history of a locality, and they were read as news or as relevant comments on the events.

Who were these poets? They were given more than one name. Some called them 'country poets' and others 'folk poets', or perhaps one of them would occasionally be referred to, in a more positive way, as the 'village poet'. They were the same ones as those who had composed the memorial poems in black frames which adorn the walls of the parlour in many Welsh cottages. The folk poet was a craftsman or farmer who followed his occupation in the area where he was born, who knew all the people in the neighbourhood and who could trace their family connections, who also knew the dialect of his native heath, and every story, event and omen, and who used the traditional social gift of poetry to console a bereaved family, to contribute to the jollifications at a wedding feast, or to record a contretemps with lightly malicious satire. His talent was a normal part of the propriety and entertainment of the Welsh rural society, chronicling its happenings, adorning its walls and its tombstones, recording its characters, its events, its sadness and its joy. It was a craft; the metres,

2

the vocabulary, the praise and the words of courtesy were traditional. It was not expected that it should be different from its kind. It was sufficient that it appropriately followed the pattern.

He proceeds to express his disappointment that the contents of the volume he was reviewing had little in common with the true folk poetry of Wales. To him, at that time, it represented a clear departure from the tradition and the role of the *bardd gwlad*:

It is sad to see that all these poets are people without kin. We do not find here a poem about a wedding or the birth of a baby . . . The kin of these poets are the mountain birds, the rainbow and the lonely places. They do not marry or give in marriage, they do not quarrel, and do not see their neighbours often enough to be satirical about them . . . I readily acknowledge their talent, for in this volume we find many beautiful poems. But it is beauty according to the pattern of the romantic prifeirdd, *and I mourn the loss of the truly unique character of the* bardd gwlad—*the poet who lived amongst his people and who composed the poetry of civilization and habitation* (cyfannedd).

Thus, the role of the folk poet is defined within a strict social context. Once he begins to sing lyrical poems about birds and rainbows and quiet places he ceases to be a folk poet. Later on we shall have to discuss why the rural poets at that time departed from the recognized folk tradition, and to what extent that trend continued in later years. At this point it suffices to say that Mr Saunders Lewis's basic definition is a fruitful starting point for our discussion. But it will be interesting to note to what extent other literary

3

critics agree with him concerning the essence of folk poetry.

In his book Y CREFFTWR AC YSGRIFAU ERAILL (pp. 40–46), the late Mr. J. M. Edwards, a poet of considerable standing, whose roots were in rural Cardiganshire, has this to say about the *bardd gwlad*:

The bardd gwlad *is a part of society. This is how it has always been, and he performs his function as a member of a rural community. It is from this neighbourly atmosphere that he draws his inspiration, not from any academic, educational or philosophical source. It is not consistent with his nature to harbour ambition or to be highbrow, nor indeed to strive for any conscious critical standard. Since the spoken word is the raw material of literature, he will have a better opportunity than many who are more literary-minded, to sustain and strengthen the stream of our traditional poetry. Williams-Parry showed through his constant love of nature, his poems to his friends and acquaintances, as well as his love for the atmosphere of the rural community, that he is the greatest folk poet of our century, and that a College post could not sever this essential and living connection between him and his early roots. Later, the poems of many others proved the very same thing. Because they had, in addition, a very high degree of respect for their craft, and artistic ability and conscience, they raised their art to a high level and a lasting one . . . The aim and condition of his (*bardd* gwlad) *work is to notice and hear the everyday happenings in the life of the folk around him, and he expresses them in a common, normal and concrete vocabulary . . . His duties are so completely and fundamentally native that he is as much a part of the pattern of his community as any other craftsman. The spoken patterns he uses are as essentially 'neighbourly' as the stones and trees of the district are in the hands of the stone-mason or the carpenter. The tendency,*

4

seen quite often today, to be ultra-literary or academic does not affect him at all. (By now the rural atmosphere has become to a great extent impure because of some unfamiliar and foreign influences.) . . . Some of the best Welsh poets in every period have been folk poets—poets with the aura of the rural community on their work as well as on their clothes. The possibility of producing a major poet with a touch of the artistry of the old 'masters' on his work recedes as education over-emphasizes other aspects and indeed concentrates on them.

This definition seems to maintain the contrast between the folk poets and the 'academic poets' (i.e. those who have received a college education), but one wonders whether the polarity is as pronounced as is suggested, within the actual situation. The advent of secondary education for all has certainly made a difference, but it has not fundamentally changed the nature of the rural community and the role of the local poet as one of its artistic interpreters.

It is interesting to note that in J. M. Edwards's definition there is one significant divergence from the view expressed by Saunders Lewis. The former specifies 'love of nature' as one of the characteristics of the folk poet, whereas the latter maintained that the *bardd gwlad* departed from his traditional subject-matter when he began to eulogize nature and the countryside. One should not be pedantic on this particular issue. A poet from a rural background would naturally sing the praises of the idyllic atmosphere, and would almost inevitably be tempted to describe such aspects as the pageant of the seasons, as so many folk poets have done. But this would be an added string to his harp and could well be described as providing the necessary accompaniment to his main themes. A *bardd gwlad* who sings the praises of the heath and heather of his native *bro* is by no means a rare phenomenon in Welsh literature.

Another worthwhile definition, which substantiates this view, has been given by Dr. R. M. Jones, Aberystwyth, in his book, LLENYDDIAETH GYMRAEG 1936–1972 (pp. 72–86). This is how he outlines the role of the folk poet:

In our days we have to tie the bardd gwlad, *in terms of subject-matter, to the land and to the agricultural world; he speaks of the world that he knows, and when he turns away from that he ceases to be a* bardd gwlad. *As for the content of his poems, the natural constituents are the world of nature, the characters in his own habitat, and the events of his own personal life. The folk poet depends, to a certain degree, on the customs of his society, for it is his role to create what is expected of him. And when he produces an 'unexpected' line or verse or poem, he is 'unexpected' in the expected way. In essence, also, the folk poet is not a revolutionary innovator; despite his ability to be original and brilliant, the formal and ideological development in his work has to take place within a pattern of normality.*

It seems to me that we have to accept the main tenets of these definitions. The primary contention is this: the term *bardd gwlad* means exactly what it says—a poet in a rural community, reflecting the character of his society, its personalities, and its varied activities, its crafts and its diverse interests. Nevertheless, we should not confine the *bardd gwlad,* in too literal a sense, to

6

an entirely rural context, for that would mean precluding poets who are, for instance, colliers or quarrymen. And there is ample justification for considering these within the classification of folk poets. The line of demarcation between the 'country poets' and the 'folk poets' is necessarily blurred at this point. But even in the case of folk poets whose immediate preoccupation is with an industrial atmosphere, there is an indirect background of rural life which moulds their vision, for their forefathers were part of the influx to the industrial belt from the agricultural areas. Today, however, when we have the third generation of descendants in the industrial zones, there are few poets who compose in the vernacular, and the rural background has ceased to hold sway.

II

How deeply-rooted in our literary heritage is the folk tradition? The poetry of Wales that has survived in manuscripts from the mediaeval period was for the most part aristocratic; it was written almost entirely for aristocrats by professional poets and aristocrats who had learnt the art.

It was, for the most part, the poetry of homage and praise to the nobility, who gave patronage to the poets, and it was noted for its evident professionalism. The court poet was jealous of his craft, and this is clearly manifested in the degree of mastery he attained when composing in the 'strict metres' or *cynghanedd*, that brand of alliterative poetry which is uniquely Welsh. *Cerdd Dafod,* as it was called, was governed by a strict system of rules, and no poet was worthy of his calling if he had not meticulously respected these rules in constructing his poems. This was the essence of the classical tradition in Welsh poetry, and that period stands out as one of the high points of Welsh literature.

The folk poet of today, on the other hand, is very much a man of the people, acknowledged by them and voicing their ideals and sentiments. And yet there are obvious links of craftsmanship and themes between the two traditions. The *bardd gwlad* of today is as well-versed in the rules of *cynghanedd* as was his predecessors, and poems in the strict metres are very often his *forte*. It is a tradition that spans the centuries, and respect for the 'old art', and increasing interest in its possibilities is one of the characteristics of the present scene in Welsh poetry, and praise or eulogy is one of the chords that is still struck, with the marked difference that the ordinary folk of the poet's community are now the subjects of that praise.

To revert to the historical development—by the sixteenth century the classical tradition was beginning to lose its virility, and in the manuscripts of that century we find a considerable number of poems different in theme and technique. This poetry is 'free verse', untrammelled by the complexities of the strict metres which had been the vogue, and the themes having a popular rather than an aristocratic appeal. It was poetry produced by the lowest order of bards called *Y Glêr,* a term derived, very significantly, from *clerici (vagantes).* Undoubtedly, it is here that we find the *bardd gwlad* emerging for the first time. The tradition of the popular 'social' poet had been established.

These 'free verse' poets, like the Bards of the Nobility, believed that poetry had a social function. They took as their subject-matter the day-by-day happenings in the life of the community in which they lived. They sang of love, sadness, joy and religious beliefs; they satirised new tendencies and fashions, or age-old social vices; they entertained with poems of humour, and they gave vivid accounts of every unusual event. It was a poetry, not for the nobleman's

9

court, but for the poet's kinsfolk and friends—
an unpretentious record of things that mattered
to the ordinary people of a rural community.

The 'free verse' poetry, at first, had none of the
complexities of the poetic art of the strict metres,
and it demanded much less discipline. Its main
virtues were directness and simplicity. It cannot
be said, with certainty, who all these poets were,
for a great many of their poems were published
without the authors' names. But there is
considerable evidence to support the view that
these were poets of the people. For one thing,
their language is much nearer to colloquial
speech than the bardic poetry. And there is in
the poems a certain atmosphere of *bonhomie*
which one would expect from a folk tradition.

Despite the fact that they were, at first, very
different from their aristocratic predecessors,
these folk poets seem to have become fascinated
by the sophistication and intricacies of the
classical bard's art, and many of them attempted
odes and long poems in the classical tradition.
This would not have been possible in an earlier
age, as the classical bard's craft was only available
to the privileged circle—usually the sons of
noblemen. But when the ancient bardic tradition
was in decline, in the sixteenth and seventeenth
centuries, what once had been regarded as the
jealously-guarded craft of a guild became known
to all who were sufficiently interested to learn.
Thus, there was a fusion of two vastly different
traditions—the love of form and poetic craftsmanship on the one hand, and the desire to make
poetry a popular means of entertainment and
edification on the other.

10

It is from this double tradition that the poetry of the *bardd gwlad* has developed during the last three hundred years. In terms of content one could equate it with the folk poetry of most European countries, but because of the unique legacy inherited from the medieval bards, characterized by a discipline in form and craft, it is folk poetry which is without parallel in any other country. The *clerici* of this period had ceased to depend on the patronage of noblemen. They were the new amateurs, and the future of Welsh poetry depended on them, for the former patrons were quickly becoming anglicized.

III

We now come to another aspect of the folk tradition in Welsh poetry—that which is found in the collection of traditional stanzas or *penillion telyn* ('harp verses') which appear mostly in the manuscripts of the seventeenth century. They are probably the remnants of a much larger oral tradition. We do not know who composed them, but without a doubt they were the work of folk poets with a rural background. In these epigrammatic poems, countryside customs and popular folk lore are often mentioned, and the traits of human nature are another recurring theme. And they often refer to the rural craftsmen, the blacksmith, the carpenter, the weaver, the tailor, the cooper, the tanner, not to mention the farmer and the miller. Weather lore and nature gnomes, festivals and fairs, animals and implements—they all come within the orbit. But perhaps the most memorable verses are those on the subject of unrequited love, which, because of their intense personal feeling, mark them out as being rather different from the traditional poems of the *bardd gwlad*.

Here are some varied examples of the *penillion telyn*:

> *O f'anwylyd, cyfod frwynen,*
> *Ac ymfael yn ei deupen;*
> *Yn ei hanner tor hi'n union*
> *Fel y torraist ti fy nghalon.*

12

(Darling, pluck a reed that quivers,
Hold its ends between your fingers,
Break it in the middle cleanly
Like you broke my heart so surely.)

Rhaid im' fyned â'm piserau
I roi llymaid bach i'r lloeau;
Ac at y fuddai fawr i gorddi
Nes bo modryb wedi codi.

(I must go now with my pitcher
To feed calves that are in hunger,
Then to do a little churning
Till my aunt will come a-stirring.)

Yn y felin mae lle difyr
Pan fo Elin dda ei natur,
Ac yn adrodd hen benillion,
Nes gwneud pawb wrth fodd eu calon.

(In the mill it is amusing
When comes Elin, so good-willing,
To recite old verses, snappy,
Until everyone is happy.)

Dacw rosys ar y bryn,
Rhosyn coch a rhosyn gwyn.
Rhosyn coch a gyll ei flodau,
Rhosyn gwyn gymeraf innau.

(I see roses on yon height,
One is red, the other white,
The red will have its petals falling,
'Tis the white rose I'll be taking.)

13

Mi weriais gant o sylltau,
Do, fil o chwecheiniogau
I yfed cwrw a gwin at Gwen
A'i cholli ar ben y siwrne.

(A thousand shillings silver
And sixpences for ever
I spent on wine and beer for Gwen,
And even then I lost her.)

There is a world of difference between these
verses, with their unassuming craftsmanship and
their direct simplicity, and the intricate alliterative poems of the previous centuries. Almost
inevitably, they later became an influence on the
work of the folk poets. For one thing, the metres
were lively and musical. The lyrical note was
another appealing feature, and this note was
often heard in the centuries after the traditional
verses had become 'accepted'. Poets like Huw
Morus (1622–1702) recognized their value and
used them as patterns for some of his poems.
The extent to which the harp verses are accepted
in our own days is exemplified in the fact that
they were the set forms for the Crown competition in the National *Eisteddfod* held at
Cardigan in 1976—and it is significant that this
was in a part of the country which had become
renowned for its folk poetry. It must be added
that these traditional verses, at least in their
form, became the basis for other kinds of folk
poetry in Wales in the late sixteenth and seventeenth centuries. Morgan Llwyd used them in his
religious exhortations, as did Richard White in
urging people to be loyal to the Catholic Church.
But the one who popularized them more than

14

anyone else was Rhys Prichard, the Vicar of
Llandovery. He composed thousands of verses
with the aim of exerting religious and moral
persuasion on his fellow countrymen.

IV

At the beginning of the eighteenth century the ordinary people of Wales were beginning to read, and soon they were seeking some literary entertainment besides the popular epigrammatic poems that had been handed down from one generation to another; they were longing for some more thrilling material. And the press at that time proved itself ready to satisfy this need by publishing ballads to be sung on well-known tunes. One way of publishing them was through the almanacks which had a wide circulation throughout the land. The various kinds of poetic efforts contained in these almanacks kindled the interest of many literary-minded people in the art of poetry, and it was material accepted with relish by the aspiring folk poets of the day. We are here close to the true explanation of the phenomenon of the rapid growth in the number of *beirdd gwlad* who ventured to publish their versifications. It is true that some of the traditional Welsh poetry was included in the almanacks. For instance, Gwilym Howel published the *cywyddau* of Goronwy Owen in them. But a great deal of the poetry took the form of ballads, many of which had a wide appeal and became well-known.

Ballads were also circulated through pamphlets to be sold at markets and fairs where they were sung. Amongst the earliest of these 'peddlers' were Evan Ellis of Llanfihangel Glyn Myfyr,

Thomas Roberts, Llanllyfni, Hugh Evans of
Llannor and Hugh Jones, Llangwm, who published his DIDDANWCH TEULUAIDD (*Family Entertainment*) in 1763. Others who became well-known
were Dafydd Thomas of Waunfawr and Walter
Davies of Llanfechain. Dr. Thomas Parry in his
book BALEDI'R DDEUNAWFED GANRIF (p. 23) drew
attention to the fact that the majority of the
ballad writers of this period came from four
valleys—Conwy, Edeirnion, Clwyd and Llan-
gollen. There were others in the South—poets
like Dafydd William, Llandeilo Fach, better
known as a hymn writer; Evan Thomas,
Llanarth; Thomas Miles, Blaenau; Evan Powell,
Llanfynydd: and at a later date, Dafydd Jones,
Llanybydder; John Thomas, Aberdare; and Lefi
Gibbon, Cwmfelin Mynach.

One should remember, however, that the tradition of the North with regard to the ballad was
different from that of the South. The ballads of
North Wales were mostly in *cynghanedd,* and their
authors did their utmost to preserve and respect
the 'old art'. Undoubtedly, they were in the
tradition of the *cywyddwyr* but with a different
purpose to their poems. Instead of entertaining
the gentry in their courts the poet was now
entertaining farm servants in the fairs. Instead of
Tudur Aled, the nobleman, singing the praises
of his proud friends we have cobblers and
weavers and blacksmiths versifying about
robberies and murder.

But the ballads of the South were not in the same
tradition—at least, not in their form. They were
in the free verse tradition, in less complicated

17

metres. It is interesting to note that many of the metres were later adopted by hymn-writers. There is considerable justification for the opinion expressed by Dr. Thomas Parry in BALEDI'R DDEUNAWFED GANRIF (p. 21) that the ballads of the North belonged to the tradition of Goronwy Owen and those of the South to the tradition of William Williams, Pantycelyn. In their different ways the ballads of both traditions left their impact on the patterns of folk poetry. When we read through the collections of poems published by the *beirdd gwlad* of our own day, we see that both strands are there—the pithy alliterative poems side by side with free verse efforts.

Why do we consider the ballad writers to be folk poets? The most significant fact is that they were mostly rural craftsmen. It is names like these that we see most often: Hugh Lloyd, the weaver; William Walter, the cobbler; Owen Roberts, the joiner; Ellis Roberts, the cooper; John Roberts, the apprentice of William Roberts the blacksmith. These were, in a real sense, the folk poets of the eighteenth century. And in the following century the even more popular ballad writer came into his own. He would be the champion of the common people, the voice of their conscience when they were the victims of injustice or oppression. And he became important as the chronicler of current events that were of more than ordinary interest in a particular locality. The social role of the *bardd gwlad* was becoming more firmly established. The subjects of the ballads varied a great deal more in the course of time. Wars, earthquakes, plagues and accidents were favourite subjects. A bad corn harvest or a scant potato crop would occasionally justify a ballad, while a gruesome murder would provide an opportunity not to be missed. And as could be expected, the 'perpetual' events of births, marriages and deaths would provide some of the material. The local poet would be expected to greet a young couple on their marriage, to offer his congratulations on the birth of a child, and to compose a memorial poem when a well-known personality passed away. This tradition has flourished through to our own times. In reality the subjects of the folk poet have not changed to a great extent since the eighteenth century, and reading through the published works of contemporary authors like Dic Jones and Dafydd Jones (Ffair Rhos), we see that this kind of poetry is an essential part of their output. They sing to their own *bro* and to their own people, sharing their joys and sorrows, providing their community with the topical ballads that form part of its literary diet.

It must be noted, here, that the poems of the present day *bardd gwlad* are more artistic and polished than the ballads of those who flourished in the eighteenth century. Most of the ballads at that time had little literary merit; they were composed to be *sung*, and they must be judged in that light. By the beginning of that century a great many popular tunes had become known to the people. But by the end of the century most ballad-singers were making use of a much narrower range of tunes.

With the passage of time, some of the ballad-singers would have an English version to accompany the Welsh one. This was especially true of those circulating in Glamorgan. One such ballad was the one to 'The Terrible Explosion at Senghenydd, near Caerphilly. Loss of 100 lives. May 24th, 1901'. Another was a ballad composed by one L. Bevan to 'The Explosion at Clydach Vale, which occurred Friday evening, March 10th, 1905'. Occasionally, a more lyrical note crept into the ballad, and the following is a typical English version, circulating in pamphlet form in South Wales towards the end of the last century:

FAR AWAY

Where is now the merry party
  I remember long ago,
Laughing round the Christmas fire,
  Brightened by its ruddy glow,
Or in summer's balmy evenings
  In the field upon the hay?
They have all dispersed and wandered
  Far away, far away.

Some are gone to lands far distant
  And with strangers made their home,
Some upon the world of waters
  All their lives are forced to roam;
Some are gone from us for ever,
  Longer here they might not stay—
They have reached a fairer region
  Far away, far away.

There are still some few remaining
　　Who remind us of the past,
But they change as all things change here,
　　Nothing in this world can last.
Years roll on, and pass for ever,
　　What is coming, who can say?
Ere this closes many may be
　　Far away, far away.

V

Another kind of folk poetry written in the eighteenth century was the 'interlude'. This was a versified play, performed on waggons in farmyards or at fairs or markets. Occasionally it was presented in a public house, with a large table as a stage. The metre used, more often than not, was the *triban*, a form usually associated with Glamorgan, a verse of four lines, of which lines 1, 2 and 4 have a common rhyme, and with an internal rhyme in the middle of line 4. Many lines had touches of *cynghanedd*. These verses from the interlude 'Tri Chryfion Byd' by Thomas Edwards (Twm o'r Nant) serve to illustrate the style of the poetry:

> *Fe ddwedodd y sarff o'r dechre*
> *Y bydde dynion megis duwie,*
> *A'r balchder hwnnw sy'n ffals ei wên*
> *Yn glynu mewn hen galonne.*

> *(Said the serpent from beginning:*
> *Men like gods will soon be reigning,*
> *This selfish pride with its false smile*
> *Is all the while in man's thinking.)*

> *Mae balchder Cymry ffolion*
> *I ymestyn ar ôl y Saeson,*
> *Gan ferwi am fynd o fawr i fach*
> *I ddiogi'n grach fon'ddigion.*

22

(Some Welsh folk are so foolish
Striving to ape the English;
Young and old are trying to be
Like gentry—what mock polish!)

The subject-matter of the interludes varied a great deal. Tales from Welsh history and Biblical stories provided popular material. Some authors took it upon themselves to give religious instruction through these plays. But the most popular of all the interludes were those presenting judgements on the kind of society which existed in those days. This was the theme of the most well-known interludes attributed to Twm o'r Nant—'Tri Chryfion Byd' *(The Three Strong Men of the World)*; 'Pleser a Gofid' *(Pleasure and Sorrow)*; and 'Cybydd-dod ac Oferedd' *(Miserliness and Vanity)*.

Who were these authors who gave their poetry dramatic form, and to what extent can we call them folk poets? Undoubtedly, they were mostly rural workmen or craftsmen. Twm o'r Nant was a 'timber carrier'; Huw Jones from Llangwm was a farm-servant, and Ellis Roberts from Llandoged was a cooper. Their purpose was to entertain as much as to instruct, and in those days people could recite parts of a well-known interlude from memory. But with the passage of time and with the growing influence of religion the interlude lost much of its appeal, and it ceased to be a literary exercise for the poet and a means of entertainment for the masses.

23

VI

We do not usually consider hymn-writers to be folk poets, and yet, we should not forget their roots in the thoroughly rural community. And we certainly should not minimize the influence they had on generation after generation of local poets, from the beginning of the eighteenth century onwards. It is true that very few of the hymns in *cynghanedd* have survived; it was people like Thomas William, Bethesda'r Fro, John Williams, St Athans, Edward Jones, Maes-y-plwm, and Ann Griffiths, Llanfihangel yng Ngwynfa, who composed the more polished hymns, and they were heavily under the influence of William Williams, Pantycelyn, and his metres. The large output of hymns at that time provided a new set of patterns for the *bardd gwlad*, and the influence can be clearly seen in the lyrical and moral poems of the nineteenth century and the beginning of the twentieth. The Methodist Revival was a most potent influence, but it hardly added to the quality of the poetry produced by the *bardd gwlad*; more often than not it simply meant that he was tempted to be other-worldly in his themes and sanctimoniously moral in his emphasis. In other words, he was in danger of becoming something other than a folk poet in the true sense of the term.

VII

In the nineteenth century there were two far-reaching influences on the folk tradition,—first of all the *Eisteddfod*, and later on, the Romantic movement.

The beginnings of the modern *eisteddfod* were in the eighteenth century, although the form at that time was rather different. The poets used to meet in taverns to vie with each other in composing *englynion*. In his book TRADDODIAD LLENYDDOL MORGANNWG (*The Literary Tradition of Glamorgan*), (the late Professor) G. J. Williams mentions a number of these events, and this is also the picture drawn by one of the great literary figures of the century, Edward Williams (Iolo Morganwg), when he describes *eisteddfodau* held at Llantrisant and other places.

Later, the local *eisteddfod* took on another pattern, and was freed from the mock professionalism of the 'tavern poets' who had sought to re-establish the old rabbinic-style code of poetic rules. The ordinary people became involved, and the interest of the folk poets was kindled in district after district. One cannot over-emphasize the impact of the *eisteddfodau* on the *beirdd gwlad*. They provided them with a new incentive, and the editor of the 'poets' column' in the local newspaper was always ready to publish their winning efforts. Apart from the regional *eisteddfodau* there were the competitive meetings, or 'penny-readings' as they were sometimes derisively called, in almost every village. These proved to be excellent nurseries for budding poets, and they helped considerably to establish poetry as one of the folk arts.

On the other hand there was the 'National' *Eisteddfod* which had grown to become one of the accepted institutions, expecially after 1789, when the *Gwyneddigion*, the London-based society of literary people from *Gwynedd*, began to take an interest in it. Their outlook at first was stubbornly traditional, not least in the choice of subjects. It is almost incredible to us today that these were the kind of subjects set: 'The Isle of Britain and its defence against enemies', and 'The visit of George IV to Anglesey'. The *Gwyneddigion* failed to capitalize on the rich bardic tradition of Wales. They knew the poetry of Milton and the 'Odes' of Pope and Thomson, and to them these were the norms for which the Welsh poets should strive. They believed, with the majority of the literary critics of Europe, that the epic, the long poem depicting the life of some hero or other, was the highest form of literature. They encouraged the poets of Wales to believe this and they offered prizes for long poems on a subject specified a year ahead. At first, the prize was for an *awdl*, a long poem in *cynghanedd*, for the *Gwyneddigion* believed that alliteration was the essence of Welsh poetry. But there were others who believed that the strict metres did not give the poets sufficient freedom when composing their heroic epics. After a period of lively discussion it was decided

26

to introduce a separate competition for a long poem in free verse, a *pryddest*.

Thus we have the pattern that is still a feature of the National *Eisteddfod*,—a chair for a poem in *cynghanedd* and a crown for a free verse effort. But it is sad to think that no great poem came from the *Eisteddfod* during the last century. The local *eisteddfodau* provided the real incentives for the folk poets. From 1860 onwards the National *Eisteddfod* was held every year, and it gradually increased its appeal to the hundreds of local versifiers throughout the country. It seemed as if the *gwerinwyr* were bringing their influence to bear on it. But by now the *Eisteddfod* was being monopolized by the 'poet-preachers', most of whom were men who had been denied the privilege of a University education, but who had received their training in the Theological Colleges. It became fashionable for ministers to be poets as well as theologians, and if one of them became a 'National Winner' his church would be all the more proud of him. At that time it was *expected* of a minister that he should take an interest in poetry.

The extent of the monopoly of the poet-preachers on the *Eisteddfod* is seen by the fact one of them was invariably appointed to be Archdruid of the *Gorsedd*, and the adjudicators for the chair and crown competitions were also chosen from among them, almost without exception at one time. But the poet-preachers were not in the true tradition of the *bardd gwlad*. The content of their poems was determined more by their vision of the ideal society than by their sense of belonging

27

to a local community. Moral and spiritual persuasion became the incentive for composing a poem, and naturally, the religious revivals were reflected in the themes of their poetry. Nevertheless, we should neither disregard their contribution to the development of the *Eisteddfod* as an institution, nor underestimate the craftsmanship of some of their best poems, especially in the strict metres.

VIII

Who were the folk poets of the last century and to what extent were they influenced by the *Eisteddfod*? In answering that question it is inevitable that we have to confine the discussion to a few from among the hundreds of *beirdd gwlad*.

In the *Eisteddfodau* held under the auspices of the *Gwyneddigion* the two most successful competitors were David Thomas (Dafydd Ddu Eryri) 1759–1822, and Walter Davies (Gwallter Mechain) 1761–1849. Of the two, it was Dafydd Ddu who had the greater influence on the folk tradition. At first, he co-operated with the *Gwyneddigion* and organized many *eisteddfodau* on their behalf. But later, his enthusiasm for the exiles waned and he ventured on his own to form literary societies and to organize local *eisteddfodau*. In these, the activities were not confined to competitions, but also included discussions on contemporary poetry, and provided an opportunity to draw attention to some of the 'metrical faults' to which some of the poets were prone. As a result, in Llŷn and Eifionydd a new generation of poets emerged, known as 'cywion Dafydd Ddu' *(The 'chicks' of Dafydd Ddu)*. Among them were quarrymen, stonemasons, farmers, coopers and other craftsmen, most of whom published collections of their poems. In the same locality another notable poet who had often been successful at the *Eisteddfod* was Robert Williams (Robert ap

Gwilym Ddu) 1767–1850, the farmer from Llan-
ystumdwy whose *englynion* became so valued a
part of the Welsh literary heritage. He also had
his protegés, one of whom was David Owen
(Dewi Wyn o Eifion) 1784–1841, another farmer
who displayed a rare talent for the sustained epic
poem, as is shown in his well-known *awdl* to
'Elusengarwch' *(Charity)*.

This pattern was repeated in district after district
throughout Wales. A circle of poets, their interest
sustained and intensified by competitions and by
fellowship with others of like propensity, and
above all through the help and instruction of the
athro beirdd (poets' teacher), who was prepared to
take pains in the task of giving them guidance.
That became the essence of the unique tradition
of folk poetry in Wales, and significantly it is still
the pattern today. The hundreds of poets whose
work appears in contemporary publications owe
their initial involvement to some local *eisteddfod*,
their abiding interest to some literary circle or
society, and the quality of their craftsmanship
to some local personality who gave them instruction in the essentials, especially in the intricacies
of *cynghanedd*.

Another area where the folk tradition flourished
in the last century was Cardiganshire, where it
was deeply rooted in the past. Several poets published volumes of their work and their contents
were avidly read and often memorized. One such
poet was John Jenkins (Cerngoch) 1825–1894,
from the valley of the Aeron, whose poems were
published in a volume entitled CERDDI CERNGOCH.
In his book AN INTRODUCTION TO WELSH POETRY

30

(p. 16) Professor Gwyn Williams tells us that *scraps of verse by the redoubtable Cerngoch are still quoted.* His poems are not of a consistently high standard by any means, but he is so typical of the *bardd gwlad* of the last century that it may be of interest to describe more fully the contents of his volume. It is a heterogeneous collection, and his range extends throughout the length and breadth of his community.

CERDDI CERNGOCH is divided into several different sections. The first contains 'Cerddi Natur' *(Nature Poems)*, including one in praise of the village of Cribyn, and another in praise of 'Quitto', a greyhound that had retrieved a wild drake from Llyn Twrch. The next section is 'Cerddi Caru' *(Love Poems)*, all of which treat the subject of love and marriage in a light vein. Then comes a section with the intriguing title 'Penillion Pendrws' *(Doorstep Verses)*, a series of 26 verses in the form of question and answer, where a lover and his party come to plead for the hand of his beloved in marriage. This is followed by 'Cerddi Cwrw' *(Beer Songs)*, not as the title suggests in praise of the beverage, but in vehement condemnation of it, and containing the inevitable description of the drunkard and his fate. Then come 'Cerddi Hela' *(Hunting Poems)*, one of which is a ballad of over 300 lines describing one successful hunt by the pack of hounds from Neuadd Fawr, a local mansion.

'I Bersonau' *(To Persons)* is the significant title of another section of the book. And in this we see how the tradition of eulogizing the gentry was still being respected. There is a poem of tribute to Lieut. Price Lewes, Llanllyr, for his bravery in

31

Africa, a poem to greet Captain Newland, Llandysul and Miss Maude of Llanllyr on their marriage, and another in praise of T. H. R. Hughes, Neuadd Fawr, for keeping a pack of hounds. But the *bardd gwlad* had greatly enlarged the circle of 'persons' who were worthy of his talent. There are light-hearted greetings to several of his friends on their wedding day, a poem to congratulate another friend who had been chosen as an adjudicator in a ploughing match, a poem composed on receiving a photograph of the home of John and Brina Davies, Spring Green, Wisconsin, and satirical verses about two friends who had 'gone to the wells' (Llanwrtyd).

The next section is entitled 'Cerddi Coffa' *(Memorial Poems)* and it is followed by a collection of 'Cerddi Moesol' *(Moral Poems)*, where the subjects range from 'Grym Arferiad' *(The Force of Habit)*, and 'Rhagrith' *(Hypocrisy)* to 'Y Wraig Rinweddol' *(The Virtuous Woman)* and 'Crefyddau'r Byd' *(Religions of the World)*. It is in this latter section that we see how greatly the local poet of the last century was influenced by the hymn-writers, especially in the choice of metres.

The next section is perhaps the most important in the book, and the most typical of the *bardd gwlad*. It consists of 105 *englynion*, many of which had won prizes in local *eisteddfodau*. But also among them are *englynion* to local personages like the blacksmith, the postman and the policeman, and a great many epitaphs to national and local notabilities. Among the other interesting subjects are 'I John Davies, Cilerwisc, yn Aredig' *(To John*

32

Davies, Cilerwisc, Ploughing); 'I Gaseg Blaenplwyf'
(To the Mare of Blaenplwyf); 'I Ofyn Help at y Gwair'
(To ask for Help with the Haymaking); 'I Darw Moel'
(To a Bald Bull) and 'Y Myglys' *(Tobacco)*.

This section shows clearly how versatile the local
poet was, and how much of an institution he had
become in the local community. It shows, too,
that Cerngoch was no mean exponent of *cynghanedd* as we can gather from the following *englyn*
in memory of a sailor lost at sea:

> *Iach hwyliodd i ddychwelyd,—ond ofer*
> *Fu dyfais celfyddyd;*
> *Y môr wnaeth ei gymeryd*
> *Ei enw gawn, dyna i gyd.*

> *(Light-hearted he sailed to return,—but despite*
> *The help of inventions*
> *The swelling ocean took him,*
> *We have his name, and that is all.)*

There are two other sections in the volume. One
is reserved for what is called 'Manion' *(Trivia)*, but
they are far from being trifles,—most of them
being *tribannau* composed on a variety of subjects,
but usually to greet friends on special occasions.
The remaining section comprises English poems,
the first of which is to 'The Marriage of Miss
Maude, Llanlear' (a local mansion):

> *Hail, hail to Captain Newland,*
> *Who takes Miss Maude for life,*
> *Today the pair are married,*
> *And now husband and wife.*

> *The Captain for a partner*
> *Searched home and far abroad,*
> *But could not find a lady*
> *So lovely as Miss Maude.*

Chorus:
> *God bless them right to steer*
> *Throughout a long career,*
> *In happiness together*
> *From Llanfair to Llanllear.*

There follows a poem to 'Autumn', which, in content and style is very similar to the many hymns composed at that period:

> *To Thee the ever-bounteous Lord,*
> *My soul, make all thy powers;*
> *He calls, and at His voice come forth*
> *The smiling harvest hours.*
>
> *Well-pleased, the toiling swains behold*
> *The waving yellow crop;*
> *With joy, they bear the sheaves away,*
> *And sow again in hope.*
>
> *Thus teach me, gracious God, to sow*
> *The seed of righteousness;*
> *Smile on my soul, and with thy beams*
> *The ripening harvest bless.*

The poetry of Cerngoch may not be of a high standard, except for some of the *englynion*, but it does show how much of a focal point in his community the *bardd gwlad* was.

There are two further points that should be noted concerning the nineteenth century. The first is the prodigious *amount* of folk poetry published. To take only one example,—a volume entitled CERDDI ERYRI, edited by Richard Griffith (Carneddog), published in 1927 but containing, for the most part, the work of poets who flourished towards the end of the last century. It covers an area from Pen-y-gwryd, in Snowdonia, to the coast, with the parish of Beddgelert as its centre. That is not a very large geographical area, but the volume contains over 200 poems by 81 poets. It is when we consider statistical facts like these that we realize the extent to which the art of poetry had been 'taken over' by the 'amateurs'.

The other point is the complete acceptance of the *englyn* as an independent form, and the change which had occurred in its style. Previously, the best *englynion* were often dignified epigrams. But during the nineteenth century the form was treated more lightly and became a vehicle for jest and satire. And this was the beginning of a trend that has continued up to our own day. It is quite impossible to assess the contribution of the *bardd gwlad* during the last hundred years without reference to the increasing use of the *englyn* as an independent metre. By now, the competition for the *englyn* is the most popular in the National *Eisteddfod*—entries sometimes numbering hundreds. Today there is a new competition, for the best humorous *englyn*, the adjudication of which is one of the greatest attractions of the Literary Pavilion. Another indication of the popularity of the *englyn*, in a totally different context, was provided by a competition in the National *Eisteddfod* of Wrexham, 1977. A prize was offered for a collection of 100 *englynion* used as epitaphs on tombstones. No fewer than 95 entries were received—a total of 9,500 *englynion,* which created a record for the *Eisteddfod.* Even after allowing for duplicates the total was in the region of 7,500. And there is no doubt that the great majority were the work of local poets, mostly from the nineteenth century.

IX

Towards the end of the nineteenth century a new note was heard in Welsh poetry. The Romantic Movement was making its influence felt. Some of the more sensitive souls began to compose more personal, sentimental poems. Early in the century Ebenezer Thomas (Eben Fardd) 1802–1863, had composed a *cywydd* to Llangybi, mourning the loss of the past,—not the past of the old mansion but the loss of his own youth and the friends of his former years. As Dr. Thomas Parry puts it (HANES LLENYDDIAETH GYMRAEG HYD 1900, p. 269):

This is a case of the familiar, unromantic things, inspiring a poem, not in themselves nor for their own sakes. They are part of the experience of the poet himself, to be enriched and gilded by memory. It was this exaltation of simple objects, making them important, appertaining to the very stuff of life, that gave to poetry a new path to tread. It is on this path that we find the lyrics of the last century, and at its end, the lyrics of the twentieth century.

It can be said that the lyrical note was first heard in the poetry of John Blackwell (Alun), 1799–1840, although the word *telyneg* was first used by Silvan Evans in 1846, when he called his book of poems *Telynegion*. Alun was influenced by the English poets of that time, as well as by the hymn-writers, and some of his poems were successful imitations of the old traditional harp verses. His themes, almost without exception, had an introvertive slant, and it is in his poetry that we see, for the first time, how the usual subjects of the *bardd gwlad* were being superseded by more personal themes.

The poet whose lyrics had the greatest influence on local versifiers throughout the country was John Ceiriog Hughes (Ceiriog) 1832–1887, the station-master who hailed from Llanarmon, in Denbighshire. The metres that he used as well as his style of expression provided models for many a *bardd gwlad*, for a period extending well into the twentieth century. It was not all conducive to the production of vibrant folk-poetry, for the treatment was often superficial and the dominant note was sentimental. Nevertheless, Ceiriog's poems were not without their virtues. For one thing, he had meant them to be *sung*, and he succeeded in establishing the kind of language which best suited lyrical poetry. It was dignified without being pompous or pretentious, and it provided a pattern to be followed by folk poets for many years. Without a doubt, his most influential composition was 'Alun Mabon', a long pastoral which ends with these verses, so typical of his style:

Aros mae'r mynyddau mawr,
Rhuo trostynt mae y gwynt;
Clywir eto gyda'r wawr
Gân bugeiliaid megis cynt,
Eto tyf y llygad dydd
O gylch traed y graig a'r bryn,
Ond bugeiliaid newydd sydd
Ar yr hen fynyddoedd hyn.

Ar arferion Cymru gynt
Newid ddaeth o rod i rod;
Mae cenhedlaeth wedi mynd
A chenhedlaeth wedi dod.
Wedi oes dymhestlog hir,
Alun Mabon mwy nid yw;
Ond mae'r heniaith yn y tir,
A'r alawon hen yn fyw.

(Still the mighty mountains stand,
Round them still the tempests roar;
Still with dawn through all the land
Sing the shepherds as of yore.
Round the foot of hill and scar
Daisies still their buds unfold;
Changed the shepherds only are
On these mighty mountains old.

Passing with the passing years
Ancient customs change and flow;
Fraught with doom of joy or tears,
Generations come and go.
Out of tears' and tempests' reach
Alun Mabon sleeps secure,—
Still lives on the ancient speech,
Still the ancient songs endure.)

One who came greatly under the influence of Ceiriog was Eliseus Williams (Eifion Wyn) 1867–1926, from Porthmadog. A clerk and accountant by profession he was inspired by the world of nature and the rural life. Different from Ceiriog he was well-versed in the art of alliterative poetry (*cynghanedd*), but it was his lyrics that influenced the local poets at the beginning of this century, especially his lyrics to the months of the year and his well-known poem to 'Cwm Pennant'. In his work the lyric became more firmly established as an accepted part of the *repertoire* of the *bardd gwlad*. At his best Eifion Wyn showed how the artistry of a poet could turn a *cliché* about the world of nature into poetry, and how an old convention could be imbued with new life.

Before the final volume of Ceiriog's poetry had been published in 1896, a type of 'new poetry' had appeared on the scene, under the influence of the work of William Thomas (Islwyn) 1832–1878. A number of the poets had applied themselves to the task of composing long free-verse poems, full of meditation about the nature of man and the purpose of creation, and especially about the relationship of man with God. This was not in the tradition of the *bardd gwlad*, for he was never a philosopher and much less a theologian.

At the end of the nineteenth century and the beginning of the twentieth yet another kind of 'new poetry' came into being. University education had provided the poets with new horizons and Celtic mythology in particular proved to be a fruitful source of inspiration. One of the first in this field was Howell Elvet Lewis (Elfed) 1860–1953. His love poem 'Llyn y Morynion' which won a prize at the Wrexham National *Eisteddfod* of 1877 caused a considerable stir, and the same kind of sensitiveness and confident craftsmanship was seen in his subsequent work, and of course, in his hymns. But despite the fact that Elfed himself hailed from the heartland of rural Wales his poems were not in the folk poet tradition.

40

Others, besides Elfed, turned to mythology for material, and the beginning of this century was one of the most stirring periods in the history of Welsh poetry. The 'College poets', the Professors of Welsh, began to publish their work,—John Morris Jones, T. Gwynn Jones and W. J. Gruffydd. But, as could be expected, the kind of material used and the poetic form given to it, did not appeal to the poets who had become intoxicated with the lyrics of Ceiriog and Eifion Wyn. Later, R. Williams-Parry, T. H. Parry-Williams and D. Gwenallt Jones came to continue the renaissance, but although more and more of the literary-minded people were becoming enamoured of the 'new poetry', it was evident that, with few exceptions, these were not the voices of the *beirdd gwlad*.

The exceptions, however, are important. We have already seen how Mr. J. M. Edwards described R. Williams-Parry as *the greatest folk poet of our century*. It is not difficult to understand the reason for such an assessment. In the work of R. Williams-Parry the poetry of Wales reaches a high-water mark, and his *awdl*, 'Yr Haf' *(The Summer)*, which won the chair at the National *Eisteddfod* of 1910, is probably the most important poem, in terms of influence, to have emanated from the *Eisteddfod*, and his sonnet 'Y Llwynog' *(The Fox)* is the most quoted sonnet in the Welsh language. His craftsmanship in the strict metres is reminiscent of the Bards of the Nobility; he is firmly rooted in the ancient bardic tradition. But he is still the poet of the people, the voice of their aspirations, the interpreter of their community. For instance, in his first volume of poems YR HAF A CHERDDI ERAILL he has no fewer than sixteen memorial poems, including his exquisite tribute (in *englynion*) to Hedd Wyn, the young shepherd-poet from Trawsfynydd, whose poem was acclaimed best and worthy of the chair at the Birkenhead National *Eisteddfod* in 1919, but who had been killed on the battlefield in France before the *Eisteddfod* took place. Other poems in the volume are tributes (albeit intensely satirical at times) to the butcher, the collier and the elderly minister, a poem to a friend about to move 'from the mountain to the village', and another to a draft of soldiers leaving for service overseas.

When the residents of the village of Mynytho in Llŷn joined together to build a village hall, R. Williams-Parry composed an *englyn* to be carved on a stone tablet on the outside wall. It is one of the most artistic examples of its kind in the Welsh language, fastidiously constructed, and yet thoroughly natural in its style of expression:

> *Adeiladwyd gan dlodi,—nid cerrig,*
> *Ond cariad yw'r meini;*
> *Cyd-ernes yw'r coed arni,*
> *Cyd-ddyheu a'i cododd hi.*

It is totally impossible to give an adequate translation of the succinct poetical content, and inevitably the music of *cynghanedd* is lost, but the gist of the thought is this: *Built by poverty, its walls are love, not stones; its woodwork is co-pledging, co-yearning constructed it.*

A typical example of the 'free verse' poem of R. Williams-Parry is his tribute to the elderly minister. It is one of a triad of poems entitled

42

'Gwanwyn' *(Spring)*, 'Haf' *(Summer)* and 'Gaeaf'
(Winter). The old minister symbolizes the winter:

> *Ti wyddost fel mae'r llanciau*
> *Mewn hiraeth am un iau;*
> *Ti wyddost am ystranciau*
> *Hynafgwyr, un neu ddau;*
> *A gwyddost ti, mor drist, mor drist,*
> *Yw diwedd oes dan groes dy Grist.*
>
> *Rhag dirmyg amlwg llanciau*
> *Mewn hiraeth am un iau,*
> *Rhag blin dristâd ystranciau*
> *Hynafgwyr, un neu ddau,*
> *Rhodded ei Feistr, o'i fawr ras*
> *Ei dirion nodded i'r hen was.*
>
> *(You know the wish of youngsters:*
> *'A younger one' than you;*
> *You know the subtle scheming*
> *Of elders, one or two,*
> *And you know too, how sad, how sad,*
> *At journey's end the cross you've had.*
>
> *But when the youth are longing*
> *For one more young than you,*
> *And when you hear the scheming*
> *Of elders, one or two,*
> *I pray the Master will uphold*
> *In grace, his servant, now grown old.)*

Later on there was to be another notable exception to the rule that the University-trained did
not write folk poetry. When R. Williams-Parry
was winning the chair for his poem 'Yr Haf' *(The
Summer)* in the National *Eisteddfod* of 1910 there

43

was a five-year-old boy in Pembrokeshire destined to become one of the most outstanding folk poets in the history of our literature. His name was Waldo Williams and after graduating in the University College of Wales, Aberystwyth in 1927 he entered the teaching profession, and was soon attracting the attention of the literary critics by the quality of his poetry and the keenness of his intellect. But it was 1956 before a volume of his poems, DAIL PREN, appeared, and it was his only published collection, although he had previously co-operated with Llwyd Williams, another Pembrokeshire poet, in bringing out CERDDI'R PLANT, a book of poems for children.

In 1977, under the editorship of James Nicholas, the Welsh volume WALDO WILLIAMS appeared, which included essays of tribute by some of his close friends and relatives, and essays of assessment by some of our foremost literary critics. Of his poetry Professor Alun Llywelyn Williams says, *Much of his published work is in the neighbourly tradition of the* bardd gwlad, *being poems to friends, or to celebrate special occasions, or lyrics eulogizing a neighbourhood and its people* . . . And this is borne out by the poems in DAIL PREN. On the one hand there are poems in *vers libre* which are remarkable for their rich symbolism and their deep mysticism. They are the product of a poetic imagination of rare quality On the other hand, there are poems which exemplify the poet's love for his native Preseli, its history-steeped culture and its good-neighbourliness. The dominant theme is always *brawdoliaeth (brotherhood)*,—the binding links of mutual kinship within a community. Friends, craftsmen, the Welsh language, rural customs and religious convictions are all within the spectrum, with the everlasting hills providing a kind of sounding-board to the clarion call of brotherhood. This is nowhere more evident than in the poem 'Preseli', the only one which he translated into English:

Wall of my boyhood, Moel Drigarn, Carn Gyfrwy,
Tal Mynydd,
In my mind's independence ever at my back;
And my floor, from Witwg to Wern and to the smithy
Where from an essence older than iron, the sparks were struck.

And on the farmyards, on the hearths of my people
Wedded to wind and rain and mist and heathery livrocky land,
They wrestle with the earth and the sky, and they beat them,
And they toss the sun to their children as still they bend.

For me a memory and a symbol—that slope with reaping party
With their neighbours' oats falling four-swathed to their
blades.
The act they took for fun at a run, and straightening their
bodies,
Flung one four-voiced giant laugh to the sun.

So my Wales shall be brotherhood's womb, her destiny she will
dare it.
The sick world's balm shall be brotherhood alone.
It is the pearl pledged by time to eternity
To be the pilgrim's hope in this little crooked lane.

And this was my window—these harvestings and sheep
shearings.
I glimpsed the order of a kingly court.
Hark! A roar and ravage through a windowless forest.
To the wall! We must keep our well clear of this beast's dirt.

X

Meanwhile there had been other developments in the field of Welsh poetry. Some of the persuasive 'poet-preachers' had produced poetry which delighted the Welsh reading public. W. Crwys Williams (Crwys) and William Evans (Wil Ifan) in particular composed lyrical poems and 'recitations' that became widely popular. They both published several volumes which were soon out of print. They were not folk poets in the strict sense of the term, and yet their work had a far-reaching influence on the local poets who were within the tradition, and their themes were less Biblical and more community-centred than their predecessors.

The work of Wil Ifan has added importance due to the fact that he became one of the first to win the National *Eisteddfod* crown for a poem in *vers libre*. This was when he won at Pwllheli in 1925 for his *pryddest* 'Bro fy Mebyd' *(My Native Heath)*, and it was a poem that had wide appeal. He was by no means an exception. Under the influence of T. S. Eliot and other English poets many in Wales reacted enthusiastically to the new vogue, especially those who had a University education. It is significant, that, almost without exception in the last forty years, the crown in the National *Eisteddfod* has been won by a poem in *vers libre*. But the trend had very little influence on the work of the many local poets, although a few of

46

them did prove that they could master the new medium.

Despite the extraneous influences and their challenge to tradition the *bardd gwlad* has steadily become a more significant figure in Welsh poetry, and especially during the last fifty years. The tradition of folk poetry has had a new lease of life, and there are several reasons for this. The 'penny-readings' and the great number of local *eisteddfodau* were revived significantly; public interest was renewed by the establishing of literary societies and poets' 'forums' in many districts. In addition, W.E.A. and Extra-Mural classes on poetry were held in many centres, and a new generation of poets emerged under the influence of tutors like Cynan, D. Gwenallt Jones, Dewi Emrys, W. D. Williams, Waldo Williams, T. Llew Jones and others. The *Eisteddfod* attracted more entries than ever from the folk poets, in particular the competition for the englyn.

At the same time the *Eisteddfod* became a kind of Mecca for the *beirdd gwlad* and personalities like Bob Lloyd (Llwyd o'r Bryn), David Jones (Isfoel) and Alun Jones (Alun Cilie) became distinct cult figures by virtue of their virile contribution to the folk culture.

In such an atmosphere the signs were promising and the folk tradition reached its zenith in our century when Dic Jones, a farmer from Blaen-annerch in Cardiganshire, Tomi Evans, a quarry-man from Tegryn, Pembrokeshire and David Jones, an agricultural officer from Ffair Rhos in Cardiganshire, three recognized *beirdd gwlad,* won the main awards at the National *Eisteddfod*. Another poet from Ffair Rhos, W. J. Gruffydd, won the crown twice, and although he was in fact a 'poet-preacher', with a distinctive style of his own, his work had its roots firmly entrenched in the folk tradition.

Another sign of the current heightened interest is the popularity of *Ymryson y Beirdd* (The Bards' Contest), where teams of versifiers compete against each other, mostly in strict metres. When it was begun in 1947 as a radio programme it did not immediately spark the imagination of the public. But early in the fifties, Sam Jones, then in charge of the B.B.C. studio at Bangor, decided to run a series of competitions between teams of poets, with R. J. Rowlands (Meuryn) as the adjudicator; public interest was soon awakened and grew apace. It was then decided to introduce the contest into the National *Eisteddfod*, and from the very beginning, at Llanrwst in 1951, it attracted large crowds to the Literary Pavilion, not on one day alone, but for two or three days of *Eisteddfod* week. At first, it was the custom to ask three or four poets to bring a team each to the *Eisteddfod*, but after a few years it was decided to organize the competition between areas or counties, and it was then that the enthusiasm welled up. Henceforth, local pride was an added incentive, although no one fully realized the significance of the fact at that time. In 1977, at the Wrexhan National *Eisteddfod*, the competition was more of an attraction than ever, with the Rev. O. M. Lloyd as adjudicator, and with exceptionally talented young poets among the competitors. And this was only one aspect of the development, for by now such contests had become a regular part of the cultural life of many districts throughout Wales. The folk tradition was reaching its maturity. And recently the success of the new magazine BARDDAS, launched exclusively to further the art of *Cerdd Dafod*, provides further proof.

There was yet another indication of the new renaissance in the number of collections of poems published by *beirdd gwlad*. Volume after volume came from the Press, representing the variety and virility of the tradition. In the sixties a series of volumes entitled 'Awen y Siroedd' *(County Poets)* was published, seven in all, between 1959 and 1964, containing the work of 453 individual poets. AWEN ARFON was the most comprehensive, with a total of 81 poets, which reflected the continuing strength of the tradition in places like Llŷn and Eifionnydd. During the same period (1959) BEIRDD PENFRO was published, containing the work of sixteen poets from Pembrokeshire. Unfortunately, no anthology was published to represent Glamorgan, Breconshire and Gwent. But recently, under the editorship of Alan Llwyd (a talented young poet from Llŷn who has emulated T. H. Parry-Williams in winning both the chair and the crown at the same National *Eisteddfod* on two occasions), a new series of volumes has appeared, entitled BEIRDD BRO, each one containing the work of some local poet of merit, mostly from North Wales.

The total number of volumes published during the last twenty-five years is in itself proof that the folk poets of Wales are reaping new harvests. Dr.

R. M. Jones, Aberystwyth, tells us that on one occasion when lecturing to a group of scholars in Quebec he drew attention to the phenomenon of the *bardd gwlad* in Wales. The scholars who heard his description of the situation confessed that they knew of no parallel, except perhaps in Iceland and Japan.

The increase in output has been matched by a greater awareness of the importance of meticulous craftsmanship in poetry. At no period in the history of Welsh literature has the *bardd gwlad* won greater recognition as an artist in his own right. Folk poetry, in the last decade or two, has occasionally reached such a high standard of execution that there is now little justification for treating the *bardd gwlad* as an amateur in his art. But he is still a folk artist in the sense that he is a social poet, reflecting the diverse facets of the community which surrounds him. In the next section I propose to deal briefly with the work of some of the 'typical' folk poets of our time, with special reference finally to the work of the circle known as the 'Cilie poets' in Cardiganshire.

XI

In 1932 a volume of poetry entitled Pitar Puw a'i
Berthynasau was published. It was the work of
one Thomas Jones, Cerrig Ellgwm, Ysbyty Ifan,
in Denbighshire, a local poet of no mean ability,
and it demonstrates the essentials of the true
folk tradition in poetry. The title itself, with the
significant word 'relatives', is an indication of the
social role of the *bardd gwlad*. T. Gwynn Jones who
edited the volume had this to say about Thomas
Jones and the district where he lived:

*The population of these neighbourhoods is scant. Some people
think that those who live in such areas do not know people, or
know very little of what goes on in the world, in comparison
with those who tread on each other's feet in the towns, and who
depend for their knowledge of people on newspapers and such
things. It is living people who are of interest to Thomas Jones,
and it is not long before he is able to measure and evaluate
them with the keenness of a master in that art.*

The titles of the poems bear this out. There are
several memorial poems, and poems to 'Pitar
Puw', to 'John Williams, Y Fron', to his grand-
daughter, to a young harpist, and to an old
hearth. The life of the whole community is
reflected and one can see how the author is
totally involved with the 'relatives' in their
comings and goings. It is the poetry of fellowship
and neighbourliness. And the poetic style is as
natural and unassuming as the life-style of the

peasants themselves. Here is how he describes 'John Williams, Y Fron':

> Dilynodd yr arad 'hyd y llethrau iach,
> A thyfai yr ŷd yn ei rychau;
> Enillai ei fwyd, gyda chyflog bach,
> A thalodd am ddillad a sgidiau;
> Yn oerni'r gaeaf ac yng ngwres yr haf
> Bu dipyn o help i'r ardal;
> Am lawer gŵr brigog gadd dywydd braf
> Ni ellir mo'r dweud pethau cystal . . .

> (He followed the plough o'er the sloping sward,
> And the corn grew in his ridges,
> He earned his food, so scant a reward,
> And paid for food and clothing;
> Through the winters cold and the summers hot,
> His neighbours he was helping,
> Of many a haughty one, luckier his lot,
> One cannot say things so pleasing . . .)

A few years after the book was published Mr. Saunders Lewis referring to the work of Thomas Jones, said:

This is what I would like to explain: that this style and its words and rhythms are eminently civilized, giving dignity to the speech patterns of the living language, the language of people in their daily occupations, but nevertheless a choice language and one appropriate to poetry. And the second point that I have is this, that the style is the very one that the poetry of Europe is seeking once again; it can be compared with the language of Lafourge and his followers in France or the language of T. S. Eliot and his followers in England. For today, closing the gap between poetry and social life is the chief aim

*of the poets of the West. The period of deliberate individualism
is over for the time being in European poetry.*

Undoubtedly, the writer of those words felt that
folk poetry was being given a new lease of life in
the work of Thomas Jones, and others like him,
and that the romanticism of the beginning of the
century was losing its appeal. Forty years after-
wards we are able to say that this trend was
continued, and that in the fifties and sixties of
this century the *bardd gwlad* attained a new stature.
Groups of poets flourished in more than one
area, their work, firmly rooted in a local culture,
giving meaningful and colourful expression to
the life of the community around them.

One such group were members of one family,
Bois y Cilie, 'Cilie' being the name of a farm near
Llangrannog in Cardiganshire. They were the
sons of Jeremiah Jones 1855–1902, a local farmer-
blacksmith who was no mean poet himself. It has
been said of the family that poetry was 'part of
their diet', and all six of the 'boys' (in a family of
twelve) showed literary talent, which was developed and sharpened by friendly rivalry in local
eisteddfodau, especially in, competitions for the
englyn. If one were to seek ample proof of the
permeating influence of a local or family culture
then the Cilie family is a patent example. The
children were imbued with the love of poetry
from the beginning and they soon became part
of the literary tradition of the neighbourhood.
The activities in that part of the world, the events
that took place, the characters who walked those
paths, their laughter and their tears,—everything

came within the range of their talent, and their poetry is a record of life as it flowed around them.

Two of the sons, Fred, 1877–1948, and Simon Bartholomew, 1894–1964, became ministers of the gospel, and were themselves talented poets, the latter winning both the chair and the crown in the National *Eisteddfod*. But it was three of the other brothers, David (Isfoel) 1881–1968, Evan George (Sioronwy) 1892–1953, and Alun (Alun Cilie) 1898–1975, who typify the work of the *bardd gwlad* in its true essence. They remained in the neighbourhood and their poetry sprang from the local soil. Isfoel was a colourful character, noted for his spontaneous humour and his talent for epigrammatic expression in verse. This was shown in an English *englyn* he composed when he was a young lad, after a young lady he had fleetingly courted had sent him her photograph:

> You are fat in your photo—yes indeed,
> Nice and tidy also,
> Sweet as jam, no sham or show,
> Ready to marry tomorrow!

It has to be remembered that when someone like Isfoel composed *englynion* in English it was for the sheer fun of it, and they were an essential part of the entertainment when they were read at a *noson lawen* or published in the poets' column of the local newspaper. But the *bardd gwlad* who became such an entertainer never ceased to be an artist, and the craftsmanship of the English *englynion* is no less meticulous than that of the poet's efforts in the vernacular.

54

A blacksmith by trade, Isfoel's poetry sparkles with effervescent wit, as is shown in his two volumes, CERDDI ISFOEL (1958) and AIL GERDDI ISFOEL (1965). But the humour itself is rooted in a sense of belonging, and the deeper note of respect for his fellow-beings is always reverberating in his lines. These collections of poems are invaluable to the social historian, for they depict life as it was in a rural area over a period of fifty years. The poems tell us of a way of life; they record the customs and delights of a people, their difficulties and their conquests, their tears and their laughter. And it is always the people who matter. But the *eisteddfod* and its competitions had a significant role in the motivation of the poet. For instance, in the first volume there are 84 individual *englynion*, most of which were probably composed for various *eisteddfodau*, and on such subjects as 'Y Ciw Bwyd' *(The Food Queue)*; 'Y Ferch Fodern' *(The Modern Miss)*; 'Crwydryn' *(Tramp)* and 'Y Bws Deulawr' *(The Double-decker Bus)*. Some of them are mock epitaphs, like the following to 'Y Morwr' *(The Sailor)*:

> Daeth hedd a diwedd mordwyo,—adieu
>   Abadan a Rio;
>   Bwciaist o Bernambiwco
>   I'th dawel draeth d'ola dro.
>
> (Now resting from your sailing, so—adieu
>   Abadan and Rio;
>   You booked from Pernambuco
>   To this beach nigh, to lie low.)

But apart from these humorous *englynion*, which very often are no more than excercises in *cynghanedd*, Isfoel's poetry contains some genuine and touching poems in memory of friends. He composed the following verse in English, as early as 1916, to one John Owen, Chief Officer of the s.s. 'Llongwen', who lost his life through enemy action on a voyage from Naples to Barry:

> I cannot bend beside his grave
> For he sleeps in the secret sea,
> And not one gentle whispering wave
> Will tell the place to me;
> But though unseen by human eyes,
> Though mortals know it not,
> His Father knoweth where he lies
> And angels guard the spot.

He could be equally effective in his tribute to the living, as in the following to one of his neighbours:

WILLIAM LLOYD

> Rhyw stacyn byr yw William
> A chadarn ar ei draed,
> Ac ynni a diwydrwydd
> Yn berwi yn ei waed.
> Ni ildia i'r dwyreinwynt,
> Ond gwasgu'n nes i'r claw',
> Can's ar y storm ffyrnicaf
> Saif William gyda'i raw.
>
> Ar feysydd y cynhaeaf
> Sopynnwr onest, gwych,
> Ac wedi'r holl lawogydd
> Bydd teisi Lloyd yn sych.
> Ped elai oriau gweithio

Ymlaen am awr neu ddwy,
Wnai hynny'r un gwahaniaeth,
Bydd William gyda hwy.

Ffeiddia'r sôn am 'gompo',
Ni ŵyr beth ydyw 'dole';
I Lloyd 'does dim yn cyfri
Ond mynnu gwneud ei ôl.
Er croesi yr Addewid
Mae'n well gan William Lloyd
Gael gweithio 'mlan am swllt y dydd
Nag uno â'r 'Unemployed'.

(A stocky man is William,
So firm upon his feet,
And in his blood flows power
And life in every beat.
He yields not to the eastwind
But seeks the sheltered lays,
For in the fiercest tempest
With shovel William stays.

Upon the harvest meadow
An honest stacker, he,
And after many downpours
Lloyd's stacks all dry will be;
And if the stint of work-day
Will stretch an hour or two,
It does not make a difference,
For William is there too.

He scorns the thought of 'compo',
He knows not what is 'dole',
What matters to Lloyd always
Is work, to do it all.
Although well past the Promise

He works on, William Lloyd,
He'd rather earn a shilling
Than being unemployed.)

The poetry of Evan George (Sioronwy) was a product of the same mould. He farmed Gaerwen, bordering on Cilie, and although he did not seem to have the sparkling versatility of Isfoel, his poems show a remarkable dedication to craftsmanship. He was evidently a well-read person, and this is reflected in the rich vocabulary which he had at his disposal. His more noteworthy efforts are contained in the volume AWEN YSGAFN Y CILIE (edited by Gerallt Jones), published in 1976. Among them are a poem in the intricate 'three beat' metre *(mesur tri thrawiad)* to 'Cwmsgog', the ruin of a local cottage, and two sonnets, the one to his father and the other to his mother. His economical style and his flair for graphic description can be seen in the following short poem entitled 'Cornicyllod' *(Lapwings)*:

Yn gawod ysgafn
  Y daethant bob un,
A'i big a'i beret
  Yn ddel eu llun.

Cri iasau rhynllyd
  Ym Mharc y Gwair,
A bore drannoeth
  Gwir oedd y gair,

Ymledai ysblander
  Yr astud len
O fanc Blaenglowon
  I fanc Gaer-wen.

(They came one evening
Like a shower light,
With their beaks and berets,
So lovely a sight.

A shivery crying
In hayfield sward,
And when came the morning
True was the word,

White splendour of silence
Like a carpet spread,
From high Blaenglowon
To Gaer-wen head.)

Nowhere is the full range of the true *bardd gwlad* illustrated better than in the poetry of Alun Cilie, the youngest of the six brothers. It was he who remained to farm Cilie for many years, and in his poetry we can sense the strong tang of the earth, and the vibrant atmosphere of the local community. When his first volume CERDDI ALUN CILIE was published in 1964, D. J. Roberts, a local minister who was the tutor of an University Extra-Mural Class which Alun had attended for years, wrote of him in the Introduction:

He had looked at nature, its scowls and its smiles, and at the people of his district in the hours of their joy and in their more solemn days, and he sang praises to the sanctuary of the things that do not perish. The hopes and longings of the neighbourhood he loved are reflected in the englynion *and sonnets we have here. In a rather important way, we have in this volume a memorial to the Welsh rural community by one who knew it well. The poet composed these poems so that the ordinary people of his locality could enjoy them. Entertaining the neighbourhood*

59

was part of the purpose. And they liked nothing better than hearing Alun Jones reading his poetry in public. To him, religion, the language and the history of a district and its people converge in poetry. It is an expression of the life of a whole community, to entertain and strengthen it.

That, in itself, is a concise description of the role of the *bardd gwlad.*

The language of Alun Cilie's poems was the living language of his native district. As Mr. T. Llew Jones wrote in a tribute at the time of his death:

He was a master of the language, although he had no schooling after fourteen years of age . . . No, his Welsh was not College Welsh but the more excellent Welsh that had penetrated the soles of his working boots into his constitution from the soil of the monoglot rural Wales, which to all purposes has ceased to exist.

Of this language Mr. Saunders Lewis said: *It is not a glove he puts on,—it is the skin of his mind.*

Another volume of Alun Cilie's poems AIL GERDDI ALUN CILIE, was published after his death in 1976. Both volumes contain a remarkable variety of poems over a wide spectrum of subjects. They illustrate the versatility of his talent and his complete mastery of the tradition. In particular, he was conscious of the almost irresistible pressures which threatened the existence of the culture of which he was such an outstanding example. This is evident in his sonnet, 'Fy Ngwedd Geffylau Olaf' *(My Last Team of Horses):*

> *Dau 'Glydesdale' gwarrog oeddynt, hoyw ac abl,*
> *A chlwstwr ceiniogau'r ceirch yn llathru'u graen;*

60

Ni ddaeth erioed eu noblach trwy ddrws stabl,
Ac ni bu gwaith a safai ddim o'u blaen.
Hyfryted gwefr y cryndod pan fai'r pâr
Yn esmwyth orwedd ar y tresi tyn,
A gorfoleddus ddilyn trwy yr âr
Yn groes i lydain rynnau'r perci hyn.
Naw wfft i gêr ddigwmni'r tractor gwych
A'u gwthiodd hwy i lawntre Pant-y-ci,
I dorden yno ymhell o rwn a rhych
A bwrw'u penolau i'r gwynt o'm gweled i;
Nes dod o'r nacer ffals, dihitio'i gnoc
Ar dor fy llaw—a'u cael am bris dau groc.

(Two arch-necked 'Clydesdales', lively and able
With clusters of bright pennies on their coats;
No nobler ever came from any stable
No others worked more willing for their oats,
So thrilling was the shiver when the pair
Lay smoothly-pulling on the harness strand,
So joyous was the feeling in the air
As we turned the wide ridges of this land.
Fie to the bright tractor's soul-less gear
Which pushed them to the fields of Pant-y-ci
Away from ridge and back, to lazy there
With backsides in the air on seeing me;
Until the crafty knacker, with cold knocks
On my palm, gets them for the price of crocks.)

Another of the Cilie poets, John (Tydu) 1883–1947, emigrated to Canada when he was a young lad, but not before he had drunk deeply of the poetic atmosphere of his home and learnt to express himself in *cynghanedd* with surprising facility. His letters home were often interspersed with *englynion* or *hir-a-thoddeidiau*. The *hir-a-thoddaid* is a verse of six rhyming lines, of ten syllables each, every line being fully alliterated, and with an internal rhyme in the middle of the last line. The construction of a *hir-a-thoddaid* demands complete mastery of the rules of *cynghanedd* but J. Tydu Jones was no novice, as these two examples prove:

WAR

A perilous night of gory fighting,
A cruel duel with brave men dying;
Invisible and horrible bombers whirring
Vineyards and barnyards and homes are burning.
A ruthless, thankless thing,—belching guns
And nations on rations hellward rushing.

PEACE

Welcome home old chap! We feel so happy
To see you again bright as a guinea;
Gone is the war and gone is the worry,
Peace is better than pieces o' booty;
By the surging, sighing sea,—in the glades
We'll live as comrades, alive is Cymru.

This is how he sang the praises of Cwmtydu, the seaside village near his home, from which he took his bardic name:

Home of the bard and the Cardi,—a mint
Of romantic beauty;
The village in the valley
Smiling by the sighing sea.

> *Leisure and deep seclusion—far away*
> *From the world's mad passion;*
> *In so lush isolation*
> *I would live and die—alone.*

The same kind of pithy phrasing is seen in his englyn to 'Spring':

> *Dew on the new-born morning,—on the heath*
> *The hawthorn is blazing;*
> *Eternal youth returning,*
> *Sprayed by the sunshine of Spring.*

At the end of the 1914–1918 War Tydu wrote a poem entitled 'The Returning Men', the last two lines of which are inscribed over the entrance to the Memorial Chamber of the Government Buildings in Ottawa:

> *All's well, for over there among his peers*
> *A Happy Warrior sleeps.*

Many of the grand-children of Jeremiah Jones also continued the tradition. One of them, the Rev. Gerallt Jones, has had a collection of poems published under the title, YSTAD BARDD. He also edited CODI'R WAL, a volume of the poems of another grandson, (the late) Mr. Fred Williams. Others who have had their poems published in various periodicals are Capt. J. Alun Jones, Capt. D. J. Williams, Mr. Jeremy Jones and Mr. Tydfor Jones, well-known for his versatility in *Ymryson y Beirdd* and in radio and television programmes. Mr. Dafydd Iwan, the 'pop' and folk singer, whose 'protest' songs created a new tradition some years ago is a great-grandson.

Of the above-named, Capt. J. Alun Jones has won the competition for the *englyn* in the National *Eisteddfod* on no fewer than three occasions. The following English *englynion* show how thoroughly he has mastered the 'old art', and how he is constantly conscious of the poet's role as an entertainer:

THE ALBATROSS

Athwart and south of 'thirty',—a glider
That gladdens our journey;
Angel of the swell is he,—
Remote and very mighty.

THE PUPPETS

Pinky and Perky, two porkers,—reeling
In frolics for viewers;
On T.V. they mime to verse
On a string lifting laughters.

IN CEYLON

Come along to Trincomalee—Ceylon,
And so load with plenty
Tons and tons of luscious tea
For your coffer or cafe.

FARAWAY PLACES

Ilo, Ilos Honolulu,—Beirut
Bahrein, Wooloomooloo,
Durban, Oran, Timaru
Adas Abab and Cebu.

That expressing themselves in verse is almost a way of life for these poets is shown by the fact that Capt. J. Alun Jones, and his cousin, Capt. D. J. Williams, both of Llangrannog, used to greet each other in *englynion* over the radio when they were voyaging abroad. Here is Capt. Jones of the S.S. 'Eskglen' greeting Capt. Williams of the S.S. 'Coralstone' a Liberty ship racing towards the Panama during the Suez war:

> *'Coralstone' alone to lee,—on the track,*
> *But the Trades are squally,*
> *Without fail gaining daily,—*
> *Bear it up, you 'Liberty'!*

and back came the reply from Capt. Williams:

> *O 'Eskglen', sail with brisk glee—the grey waves*
> *With grace and efficiency,*
> *So fair you'll beat its fury,*
> *Well-manned you'll make land and lee.*

Another poet from the same part of Cardiganshire as *Bois y Cilie*, and who was closely associated with them, is Mr. Dic Jones, the farmer from Blaenannerch. He was greatly influenced by the friendship and guidance of Alun Cilie, and also by the encouragement of Mr. T. Llew Jones, a local schoolmaster who had married into the Cilie family, and who had won the chair at the National *Eisteddfod* on two occasions. Dic Jones himself won the chair at the National *Eisteddfod* of Port Talbot, 1966, with an *awdl* entitled 'Cynhaeaf' *(Harvest)*. This poem, more than any other in our time, illustrates the new professionalism attained by the *bardd gwlad*.

65

The significance of Dic Jones's work is the quality of his technique. His choice of word, his turn of phrase, as well as his skill in the strict metres give him the stature of one of the bards of the nobility, a Dafydd ap Gwilym abroad again in his native Dyfed. The comparison with Dafydd is not inappropriate, for we have in his work the same impish humour, allied to the same sure crafts-manship. This is clearly illustrated in the few English *englynion* Dic Jones has composed. Here he is, to begin, in a more solemn mood:

THE NIGHT

No hymn of birds, no tremor—save the sounds
Of the sea's sad tenor,
The stars ascend in splendour
And the dark creeps round the door.

But the majority of the English *englynion* are in a lighter vein:

EPITAPH TO AN IDLER

He was born to laze abed,— always idle
His arms were enfolded,
He sat and never sweated
For fear of chill, still he's dead.

THE MINIATURE POODLE

Astern of the modern miss,—a bow-wow
Semi-bald I notice,
A special of the species,
The hound of the big-wig this.

PHIL BENNETT

Very cool, he's clever, quick,— an out-half
    With the touch of magic,
  A neat catch, a pin-point kick,
  Bennett is all bionic.

This last *englyn* is sufficient proof of the artistic quality of the poetry,—the comprehensive description, the pithy expression and the remarkable aptness of the alliteration. It can only be appreciated by someone who is fully conversant with the intricacies of *cynghanedd*. But Dic Jones is capable of adapting his style to fit the occasion as in the following 'Epitaph to a Farmer':

  He no more will reap and mow—no sprightly
      Filly will he follow,
    Coaxing his warring harrow
    Where the weeds and reeds did grow.

  Seafarers o'er his furrows—will no more
      Tell en masse, their sorrows,
    Nor speed, swath-sillied swallows
    O'er his grave, nor curious crows.

  In memoriam, tomorrow—abundance
      Will abound his meadow.
    And the dell will wear yellow
    To applaud his patient plough.

The compound adjective 'swath-sillied' to describe the swallows over a mown hayfield is a cogent example of the delightful originality of a poet who is not content with any hackneyed way of conveying what he observes.

He is no less at home when he composes in 'free verse', and the *bardd gwlad* is thoroughly true to his background and to the essence of the poetic tradition when he pays tribute to a departed neighbour. There is no flourish in this poem, and no unnecessary embellishments; it is the genuine expression of sadness, the voice of the community that has sustained a loss:

TREFOR

Ni waeth i mi eleni
Heb fynd i Ffynnon-fair
Yn un o'r criw i ddyrnu
Na helpu gyda'r gwair,
Oblegid bylchodd angau
Senedd y sgubor fawr,
Nid yr hen Drefor claear
Sy'n ffermio yno'n awr.

Gyrrodd ei swch i'r gwndwn
A'r oged yn ei phryd,
A hau cyn Sadwrn Barlys
'Run fath â ni i gyd.
Gwelodd Ffair Fedi lawen
A'r grynnau'n talu'n hael,
A dysgodd godi'r rhastal
Ar ambell flwyddyn wael.

Ni chlywais 'mono'n achwyn
Na chanmol chwaith ei fyd,
Dim ond i bethau weithio
Yn oilin, dyna i gyd.
A phe bai'r farchnad weithiau
Yn llac yn nhred y lloi,
Cyhoeddai'n well na phregeth
Fod y rhod yn siwr o droi.

Fe'i pasiech yn ddisylw
Yn un o dri mewn mart,
Ond gwelais e'n dod adref
Yn Gigli yn ei gart.
Anwiredd fyddai'i alw'n
Wladgarwr brwd na sant,
Ac eto 'roedd y delyn
A chwrdda yng ngwaed ei blant.

Camodd ei dir gan dybied
Y rhoddai iddo raen,
A'i adael ar ei hanner
Fel llawer un o'i flaen,
A gwn, pe câi ddychwelyd
I'r daith a gerddodd gynt
Na cheisiai ddim ond digon
I'w gynnal ar ei hynt.

('Tis well that I'm not going
To Ffynnon-fair this year
To help them with the harvest
And with the threshing there,
For death has breached the company
That in the barn gave hand,
And Trefor, so cool-headed,
No longer farms the land.

He drove his plough through meadow
And harrowed every year,
To sow by Barley Saturday
Like all of us round here,
He had some happy Autumns,
Fields cropping as they should,
But learnt to raise the hay-rack
When harvests were not good.

I did not hear him moaning
Nor gloating at his share,
As long as circumstances
Were middling over there.
And when the calves at market
Fat profits did not earn,
He'd say, just like a preacher,
'The wheel is sure to turn.'

He'd pass by quite un-noticed,
One of a group in mart;
I saw him oft, returning,
A Gigli in his cart,
He was no earnest patriot,
No saint, for all his pains,
But love of harp and chapel
Were in his children's veins.

He tramped his acres hoping
To change them more and more,
But left the task unfinished
As many men before.
I know that should he travel
This path again one day,
He'd only ask sufficient
To help him on his way.)

Dr. R. M. Jones, Aberystwyth, in his volume
HANES LLENYDDIAETH GYMRAEG 1936–72, deals with
the significance of Dic Jones and other 'local'
poets of the same calibre:

When we consider folk poets like Dic Jones, Alun Cilie and
Isfoel, poets who are thoroughly cognizant with the Welsh
bardic tradition and are adept masters of the poetic art, we
cannot but notice first of all, I believe, that this mastery of the

tradition, by itself, has given a great deal of excellence to their work, quite apart from the individual stamp which is expressed through it by the poets themselves. By virtue of the the fact that the tradition itself is a very live and present one, breathing through their work, talented poets like these are able to climb on the shoulders of the past . . . Side by side with men of comparable inherent talent, these poets, because of the greatness of the tradition in them, are able to create a literature which has to be evaluated on higher levels . . . My point is this: because he (Dic Jones) is writing from the midst of the bardic tradition, and that in a most living way, this element must be considered important in his work. Compared with a contemporary novelist, who breathes a much thinner tradition, he has incalculable advantages: it is like an adult side by side with a child . . . I have heard the expression 'Bards' Contest Stuff' (Ymryson) *applied derogatorily to the work of* beirdd gwlad *of this kind,—their* englynion *for example. That again is a misunderstanding of the value and uniqueness of the 'Contest'* (Ymryson), *and the kind of thing which makes it possible, quite apart from being a misunderstanding of the wonderful tradition associated with it. That, too, is the result of thinking of a particular poet as 'he who farms over there', rather than as one who is the special interpreter of a princely tradition. It is natural to belittle a tradition because it is so familiar and so close to us, but in fact we in Wales have been wonderfully endowed with a tradition which is unique, and one which can be thrillingly productive in the work of the poets who inherit it.*

So the wheel has taken a full turn; the 'old art' has new exponents, and the *bardd gwlad* has come of age in Welsh literature.

A Selected Bibliography

FOLK POETS

Telyn Y Dydd (Editor: Annie Ffoulkes). Caerdydd, William Lewis, 1918.

Beirdd Ein Canrif I and II. Aberystwyth, Gwasg Aberystwyth, 1934.

Hen Benillion (Editor: T. H. Parry-Williams). Aberystwyth, Gwasg Aberystwyth, 1956.

Jones, David: Cerddi Isfoel. Aberystwyth, Gwasg Aberystwyth, 1958.

The series Barddoniaeth y Siroedd (compiled by various authors). Llandybïe, Llyfrau'r Dryw, 1959 to 1964.

Presenting Welsh Poetry (Editor: Gwyn Williams). London, Faber and Faber, 1959.

Jones, Dic: Agor Grwn. Abertawe, Gwasg John Penry, 1960.

The Oxford Book of Welsh Verse (Editor: Thomas Parry). Oxford, Clarendon Press, 1962.

Jones, Alun J.: Cerddi Alun Cilie. Abertawe, Gwasg John Penry, 1964.

Jones, David: Ail Gerddi Isfoel. Llandysul, Gwasg Gomer, 1965.

THE PENGUIN BOOK OF WELSH VERSE (translated by Anthony Conran). Penguin Books, 1967.

Jones, Dic: CANEUON CYNHAEAF. Abertawe, Gwasg John Penry, 1969.

POETRY OF WALES 1930–1970 (Editor: R. Gerallt Jones). Llandysul, Gwasg Gomer, 1974.

AWEN YSGAFN Y CILIE (Editor: Gerallt Jones). Llandysul, Gwasg Gomer, 1976.

THE OXFORD BOOK OF WELSH VERSE IN ENGLISH (Editor: Gwyn Jones). Oxford, Clarendon Press, 1977.

The series BEIRDD BRO (Editor: Alan Llwyd). Abertawe, Christopher Davies, 1976 to 1978.

Y FLODEUGERDD ENGLYNION (Editor: Alan Llwyd). Abertawe, Christopher Davies, 1978.

Jones, Dic: STOROM AWST. Llandysul, Gwasg Gomer, 1978.

Historical and Critical

Bell, I. C.: A HISTORY OF WELSH LITERATURE, translated from Thomas Parry's HANES LLENYDDIAETH GYMRAEG HYD 1900 (Caerdydd, Gwasg Prifysgol Cymru, 1944).
Oxford, Oxford University Press, 1955.

Edwards, J. M.: 'Lle'r bardd gwlad yng Nghymru heddiw'. LLAFAR, Haf 1954.

Edwards, J. M.: 'Y Bardd Gwlad'. Y Crefftwr ac Ysgrifau Eraill, Abertawe, Christopher Davies, 1976.

Jones, Gerallt: 'Barddoniaeth Isfoel'. Y Cardi, Mawrth 1969.

Jones, R. M.: 'Y Norm', 'Y Bardd Gwlad', 'Bois y Cilie'. Hanes Llenyddiaeth Gymraeg 1936–1972, Llandybïe, Christopher Davies, 1975.

Lewis, Saunders: 'Prifeirdd neu Feirdd?'. Y Faner Mawrth 22, 1939.

Jones, Tegwyn: Tribannau Morgannwg, Llandysul, Gwasg Gomer, 1976.

Lewis, Saunders: 'Beirdd Gwlad'. Y Faner, Medi 25, 1940.

Parry, Thomas: Baledi'r Ddeunawfed Ganrif, Caerdydd, Gwasg Prifysgol Cymru, 1935.

Williams, Waldo: 'Bardd Gwlad'. Y Genhinen, Rhif 15.

Williams, Gwyn: An Introduction to Welsh Poetry, London, Faber and Faber, 1953. This volume contains an appendix giving a detailed description of the nature and 'rules' of the Welsh 'strict metres' (cynghanedd).

Williams, W. D.: 'Agor Grwn'. Barn, Rhifau 74–79.

Acknowledgements

I wish to express my sincere gratitude to the following:

To Dr. Stephen J. Williams for reading the essay and suggesting some improvements; to Mr. Gareth O. Watts and Mr. Richard Huws of the National Library of Wales, and Mr. Derwyn Jones, Bangor, for valuable assistance; to Mr. Victor H. John for permission to make use of his unpublished essay, 'Bardd Gwlad—A Poet and his Community'; to the Oxford University Press for permission to use 'Epilogue to Alun Mabon' from THE DEVELOPMENT OF WELSH POETRY by H. I. Bell (1936); to Gwasg Gomer, Llandysul, for permission to include 'Preseli' from DAIL PREN by Waldo Williams, and to Miss Dilys Williams for permission to use the translation of this poem; to Tŷ John Penry, Swansea, for permission to include poems from AGOR GRWN and CERDDI CYNHAEAF (Dic Jones) and CERDDI ALUN CILIE; to the authors whose poems I have included, and to the writers from whose works I have used quotations in the text; to the Rev. Gerallt Jones for some helpful suggestions; to Capt. J. Alun Jones for assistance in obtaining copies of the English poems composed by the Cilie family; to Mrs Jean Williams for typing the copy; to Mr. Daniel Huws of the National Library of Wales for reading the proofs.

The Author

W. Rhys Nicholas was born in Tegryn, Llan-
fyrnach, Dyfed. He was educated at a private
Preparatory School in Newcastle Emlyn, the
University College, Swansea, where he graduated
with Honours in Welsh, and the Presbyterian
College, Carmarthen. A Congregational minister,
he has served churches at Bryn, near Llanelli,
Horeb and Bwlch-y-groes, near Llandysul, and
Porthcawl, where he lives at present. He has
published several books, including one collection
of poems, CERDD A CHAROL. He is one of the
editors of Y GENHINEN, and has also edited BEIRDD
PENFRO, TRIONGL/TRIANGLE and CERDDI '77.

This Edition,
designed by Jeff Clements,
is set in Monotype Spectrum 12 Didot on 13 point
and printed on Basingwerk Parchment by
Qualitex Printing Limited, Cardiff

It is limited to 1000 copies of which this is

Copy No. 943

British Library Cataloguing in Publication Data

Nicholas, William Rhys
   The folk poets.—(Writers of Wales; 0141-5050).
   1. Welsh poetry — History and criticism
   2. Folk poetry, Welsh — History and criticism
   3. English poetry — Welsh authors — History
   and criticism 4. Folk poetry, English — History
   and criticism
   I. Title   II. Welsh Arts Council   III. Series
   891.6'6'1009   PB2231
   ISBN 0-7083-0709-4